The 21 l
Powerful Miraculous
Prayer

Prayer and Fasting Program for Spiritual Warfare, Deliverance & Breaking Yokes Any Time of The Year

CHUKWUEMEKA ONUORAH

<u>Copyright Page:</u>

Title: THE 21 DAYS POWERFUL MIRACULOUS PRAYERS: CHUKWUEMEKA ONUORAH

TABLE OF CONTENTS

INTRODUCTION

The Power of 21 Days - A Journey to Miraculous Prayer

David was a man living in the city of Hapeville, who was burdened by life's challenges, he stumbled upon a book titled "21 Days of Miraculous Prayer." Intrigued, he embarked on a 21-day journey of faith. Immersed in its sacred words, David poured his heart into each prayer, surrendering his worries to the divine.

Within weeks, remarkable shifts occurred. Relationships healed, financial burdens lifted, and guidance emerged amidst life's storms. But the greatest blessing was David's own transformation. Doubts dissolved, replaced by self-love and acceptance. He connected with an infinite source of grace, unlocking his true potential.

With gratitude, David witnessed miracles unfold, tracing them back to the sacred prayers that had become his companions. Now, dear reader, we present this prayer book—a guide to your own 21-day journey. Experience the power of these sacred prayers, infusing them with your authentic voice.

Embark on this journey with faith, ready to witness extraordinary miracles. Within 21 days lies the potential to unlock the doors to your divine destiny, embracing blessings, abundance, and a profound connection to boundless love.

This **21 Days of Miraculous Prayer** is a power pack that Breaks any kind of Yokes through Divine Intervention and intersession.

What is it, that has been given you sleepless night; what is that yoke that has been weighing you down; the word of God says, *"come to me all ye that labor and are heavy laden and I will give you rest. Take my yoke upon you… for my yoke is easy and my burden is light" (Mt 11:28-30)* cast your fear on him

In the depths of every believer's heart, there is a longing for freedom from burdens. Inspired by the Bible's timeless wisdom, the "21 Days of Miraculous Prayer" is a divine gift to help believers break the yokes that oppress them. *Isaiah 10:27* assures us that burdens can be lifted and yokes destroyed by the anointing. *Matthew 11:28-30* invites us to find rest by surrendering our burdens to Jesus. This prayer book serves as a roadmap, leading believers on a transformative journey of faith and liberation. Through intentional prayers guided by scripture, we lay our burdens at Jesus' feet and experience the miraculous power of His love and grace.

Join us on this sacred journey, opening your heart to receive miraculous blessings and break free from the yokes that bind you.

Breaking Free: Deliverance from the Bondage of Darkness

Dear Friends in Christ,

In the journey of life, many of us find ourselves ensnared by the invisible chains of darkness, weighed down by burdens too heavy to bear. We face battles we never asked for, struggling against forces that seem beyond our control.

But I want you to know today that there is hope. There is a way to break free from the bondage of the devil, to cast aside the shadows that have held you captive for too long through Christ Jesus who died on the cross of Calvary that you and me be saved.

It begins with faith. Believe that you are not alone in this fight; that He who have given his life for your sake is with you. The power of the Divine is with you, waiting for you to call upon Him - Jesus.

It continues with courage; knowing fully well that Christ have equipped you to trample upon devil and his agents. Face your fears head-on, for they lose their grip when exposed to the light of your determination.

It thrives on love. Love for God, love for yourself, love for others, and love for the world around you. Love is a power tool that conquer even the darkest of forces.

Remember, you have the strength within you to overcome. No matter how deep the pit or how daunting the chains, you can rise. You can break free. You are an overcomer, more than a conqueror through Christ Jesus who saved us.

Embrace the power of prayer, seek the guidance of the Divine, and surround yourself with love and positivity. Together, we can all find deliverance from the bondage of the devil.

Each new day is a chance for rebirth and transformation. Seize it with hope, faith, and unwavering determination. You are stronger than you think, and the dawn of deliverance awaits you.

The Holy Ghost Encounter: Liberation from the Devil's Captivities

Dear Seekers of Truth,

In the grand tapestry of our existence, there exists a profound spiritual encounter that has the power to liberate and deliver us from the snares of the evil one. It's a divine rendezvous with the Holy Ghost, an encounter that transcends earthly limitations and catapults us into the realm of the miraculous.

The Holy Ghost Encounter is not a mere event; it is a transformational journey of the soul. When you open your heart and invite the Spirit of the Divine into your life, an extraordinary unfolding occurs.

Liberation: The Holy Ghost, as the embodiment of God's presence, brings with it an undeniable sense of liberation. It sweeps through the corridors of your heart and soul, breaking the chains that have held you captive. It shatters the darkness that has concealed your true self.

Peace: In the presence of the Holy Ghost, you find a peace that surpasses all understanding. The turmoil of the world and the whispers of the evil one no longer have power over your spirit. You are wrapped in the serenity of divine grace.

Strength: As you yield to the Holy Ghost, you discover a wellspring of inner strength you never knew you possessed. It empowers you to resist the temptations and snares of the enemy. With this newfound strength, you become a warrior of the light.

Transformation: The encounter with the Holy Ghost is nothing short of a spiritual rebirth. Old habits, destructive patterns, and the influences of the evil one begins to lose their grip. You are transformed, renewed, and made whole.

In this sacred encounter, you are no longer bound by the devil's captivities and snares. Instead, you are set free to walk in the light of divine truth and love.

Embrace this journey with an open heart and a willing spirit. Seek the Holy Ghost's presence through prayer, meditation, and a sincere desire for a deeper connection with the Divine. Your encounter with the Holy Ghost awaits—a powerful, liberating, and life-changing experience.

May your spirit soar in the presence of the Holy Ghost, breaking free from the chains that once bound you and walking in the glorious freedom of divine grace in Jesus' name.

Encountering Christ: The Path to Building Unshakable Faith

Dear Fellow Pilgrims,

In the journey of faith, there exists a transformative encounter that stands as the cornerstone of our spiritual foundation - the encounter with Christ. It is in this divine meeting that we embark on a profound journey towards building an unshakable faith.

Step 1: Seek with an Open Heart

To encounter Christ, we must open our hearts wide, like a door waiting to be flung open. Approach this journey with humility and a sincere desire to know Him. Be ready to cast away preconceived notions and prejudices.

Step 2: Experience His Presence

Christ's presence can be felt in the quiet moments of prayer, in the beauty of nature, and in the kindness of fellow souls. Pay attention to the subtle whispers of His grace in your life. These are the moments that begin to weave the fabric of your faith.

Step 3: Immerse in His Word

In the scriptures, we find the living words of Christ. Dive into His teachings, for they are the blueprint of faith. As you read, reflect, and meditate upon His words, you'll discover a profound understanding of His character and purpose.

The 21 Days Powerful Miraculous Prayer

Step 4: Prayer as a Bridge

Prayer is the bridge that connects our hearts to Christ's. In prayer, we converse with Him, lay our burdens at His feet, and seek His guidance. Through prayer, we build a personal relationship with Him, strengthening our faith day by day.

Step 5: Embrace Trials as Opportunities

In life's trials and tribulations, our faith is tested and refined. These moments are opportunities to draw closer to Christ, to lean on His strength, and to witness His miraculous work in our lives.

Step 6: Community and Fellowship

Surround yourself with a community of believers who share your faith journey. Together, you can uplift, encourage, and support one another. Christ often reveals Himself in the love and unity of His followers.

Step 7: Share Your Testimony

Your encounter with Christ is a testimony of His grace and love. Share it with others. Your story may inspire and guide someone else on their own journey of faith.

In encountering Christ, our faith is not built on shifting sands but on the solid rock of His presence and truth. It becomes unshakable, unwavering, and enduring.

May your journey be blessed with profound encounters with Christ, and may your faith shine as a beacon of light to guide your path and inspire others.

Knowing the Word of God: Connecting Challenges to His Word in Prayer 🙏

Dear Seekers of Truth,

In the intricate tapestry of our lives, the Word of God stands as a guiding light, a source of strength, and a transformative force. One of the most powerful ways to navigate life's challenges is by knowing the Word of God intimately, connecting your trials and tribulations to His Word, and declaring His promises as you enter into prayer.

Step 1: Know His Word

To know the Word of God, you have to immerse yourself in the studying of the bible. Read and study the scriptures, not as mere text, but as living wisdom and divine guidance. Understand His teachings, His promises, and His character. The more you know, the more effectively you can apply His Word to your life.

Step 2: Connect Challenges to His Word

As you encounter challenges, seek solace and guidance in His Word. Reflect on how the scriptures apply to your situation. His Word contains timeless truths that can illuminate even the darkest paths. Find verses that resonate with your struggles and dreams, and let them be your anchor.

Step 3: Declare His Word in Prayer

Prayer is the channel through which you communicate with God. When faced with challenges, bring His Word into your prayers. Declare His promises with unwavering faith. When you align your petitions with His Word, you tap into the reservoir of His divine power.

Step 4: Watch His Word Come Alive

As you declare His Word in prayer, watch how it comes alive in your life. Doors will open, strength will surge, and solutions will emerge. His Word is not empty; it is filled with transformative power. Trust that His promises will be fulfilled in His perfect time.

Step 5: Live It Daily

Living by the Word of God isn't limited to moments of crisis; it's a daily practice. Apply His teachings to your life, letting His Word guide your choices, actions, and attitudes. In doing so, you create a life that is firmly rooted in His truth.

Step 6: Testify to His Faithfulness

As you witness the Word of God coming to life in your challenges and prayers, share your testimonies with others. Let your stories of His faithfulness encourage and inspire fellow seekers to keep faith on their own journeys.

By knowing, connecting, declaring, and living the Word of God, you unlock a powerful spiritual tool to navigate life's challenges. His Word becomes a lamp to your feet and a light to your path (*Psalm 119:105*), guiding you through every season of life.

May your connection with His Word deepen, and may your prayers be a declaration of faith grounded in His eternal truth, in His Word and by His grace,

Conquering Fear with the Power of the Holy Spirit

Dear Beloved,

Fear can be an oppressive force, one that seeks to paralyze our hearts and hinder our progress. Yet, in our faith and reliance on the power of the Holy Spirit, we have the means to conquer fear and step boldly into the life that God has designed for us.

The Source of Power: The Holy Spirit

Acts 1:8 reminds us that we shall receive power when the Holy Spirit comes upon us. This divine power is not merely a force; it's a transformative presence that resides within us, empowering us to face our fears with courage.

Identify Your Fears

To conquer fear, we must first identify it. Acknowledge the specific fears that have taken root in your heart. Whether they are fears of the unknown, failure, rejection, or anything else, bring them into the light.

The 21 Days Powerful Miraculous Prayer

Prayer and Surrender

Surrender your fears in prayer. Pour out your heart to God, acknowledging your anxieties and asking for His guidance and strength. As you surrender your fears to Him, you open the door for the Holy Spirit to work within you.

Claiming God's Promises

The Bible is replete with promises of God's protection, guidance, and love. Memorize and meditate on these verses. Claim them as your own. For example, *Psalm 23:4* says, "Even though I walk through the darkest valley of death, I will fear no evil, for you are with me."

Renew Your Mind

Romans 12:2 encourages us to be transformed by the renewing of our minds through the word of God. Replace fear-based thoughts with God's truth. Let the Word of God shape your thinking, reminding you of His love and faithfulness.

Stepping into Courage

Courage isn't the absence of fear; it's the willingness to move forward despite it. With the Holy Spirit as your guide, take small steps to face your fears. Each step is a testimony to God's transforming power.

Community and Support

Surround yourself with a supportive community of faith. Share your fears with trusted friends and mentors who can pray with you and provide encouragement.

Celebrate Victories

As you conquer each fear, celebrate the victories, and give glory to God. These triumphs become milestones on your journey of faith.

Remember, with the Holy Spirit's power within you, you have the capacity to conquer fear, step into courage, and fulfill the purpose God has for your life. Let your faith be greater than your fear, and watch as God's transformative love carries you through the power of the Holy Spirit, in Jesus Mighty Name, Amen

Spiritual Warfare: Breaking Yokes with Biblical Foundations

Dear Soldiers of Faith in Christ,

In the grand epic of spiritual warfare, our battles are not against flesh and blood, but against the powers of darkness in the spiritual realm (*Ephesians 6:12*). But take heart, for as we engage in this divine conflict, we are armed with the very Word of God—a weapon mighty enough to break every yoke that binds us.

Understanding the Spiritual Battle

In *2 Corinthians 10:4*, it is written: "For the weapons of our warfare are not of the flesh but have divine power to destroy strongholds." Our spiritual battles are not fought with earthly might but with the divine power of God.

The Armor of God

Ephesians 6:11-17 illuminates the armor of God that fortifies us in our spiritual warfare:

Truth: Gird yourself with the truth of God's Word, for it dispels the lies of the enemy.

Righteousness: Clothe yourself in the righteousness of Christ, which breaks the yoke of guilt and sin.

Gospel of Peace: Let the gospel be your footwear, providing stability and breaking the yoke of unrest.

Faith: Hold up the shield of faith to quench the enemy's fiery arrows, breaking the yoke of doubt.

Salvation: Wear the helmet of salvation, guarding your mind and breaking the yoke of eternal separation from God.

Word of God: Wield the sword of the Spirit, which is the Word of God, to declare victory and break every yoke of bondage.

The Power of Prayer

James 5:16 reminds us: "The prayer of a righteous person has great power as it is working." Prayer is our direct line to the Almighty. It empowers us to break yokes and intercede for others in their spiritual battles.

Community and Support

Hebrews 10:24-25 urges us:

"And let us consider how to stir up one another to love and good works, not neglecting to meet together." Find strength in a community of believers who can provide support, encouragement, and accountability.

Testimony and Victory

Revelation 12:11 declares: "And they have conquered him by the blood of the Lamb and by the word of their testimony." Your victories in spiritual warfare become powerful testimonies, shining as beacons of hope for others.

As we engage in spiritual warfare, we do not fight alone. We stand as soldiers of the Most High God, armed with the power of His Word, His love, and His grace. Through His Word and by His Spirit, we break every yoke that seeks to bind us, finding ultimate liberation in Christ.

Stand firm, soldiers, for victory is assured, in the mighty and unchanging name of Jesus Christ.

IDENTIFYING YOUR BATTLE

ONE-HOUR VIGIL PRAYERS PRAY BETWEEN 12 A.M. - 1 A.M., 1 A.M.- 2 A.M., 2 A.M.- 3 A.M.

And can be used any time of the day as the spirit leads.

SCRIPTURE READINGS: *GENESIS 14:15; JUDGES 7:19; EXODUS 12:12*; READ *EPHESIANS 3:20; GENESIS 32:21-30*. There are two main battles; the night battles and the day battles! Which one is your battle? ABRAHAM FOUGHT AT NIGHT AND LOT WAS RELEASED; *Genesis 14:15*. THE GIDEON'S ARMY FOUGHT NIGHT BATTLES; *Judges 7:19* shows the strategy Gideon and his warriors employed. they chose the <u>middle watch</u>, which is around 3 a.m. according to Romans (*Mt 14: 25*), when the night was cloaked in its deepest darkness. With trumpets and pitchers, they releasing a thunderous sound and a radiant light that struck fear into the hearts of the enemy.

You case cannot be different for the Lord said "..*I will contend with those who contend against you*" *Isaiah 49:25*. So, bring it to the foot of Jesus where deliverance is assured and he will set you free.

You have to make up your mind on which battle you want to fight; the hour, days or weeks. Certainly, some strongholds can only respond to Night Battles!

The 21 Days Powerful Miraculous Prayer

Child of God, step into this prayer package with unyielding faith, knowing that the battle is already won. You are not just a conqueror; you are more than a conqueror through Christ who strengthens you. The forces that oppose you will tremble at your presence as you unleash the power within you. Rise up, for the darkness cannot extinguish your radiant light.

The victory is yours!

TYPES OF FASTING

1. 24 hours fasting -Joel 1:14, 2 Sam 1:12

2. 3 days fasting -Esther 4:16, 1 John 3

3. 7 days fasting -2 Sam 12:16-18, 1 Sam 3:13

4. 10 days fasting -Acts 2:2, Acts 1:3-6

5. 14 days fasting -Acts 27:33

6. 21 days fasting -Dan 10:2, 12-13

7. 40 days fasting -Exodus 34:28, Deut 9:9-18, 1 Kings 18:7-8 Matt 4:2, Luke 4:2.

8. Above 40 days fasting -as led by the Spirit.

NOTE: NO TEARS, NO TRIUMPH!

JUST BEFORE YOU FAST

1. Get a desire. **WRITE YOUR PRAYER POINTS DOWN**. There must be a reason for your fast. See *Isaiah 58:6*.

2. Get your promises ready. See the Unfailing God's Promises pages of this book (**on page 60**). Link a promise to every prayer request. **THE WORD ATTACHED TO YOUR PRAYERS ACCELERATES YOUR ANSWERS!**

3. Start cutting down on your food intake now. Start eating light food just a few days before your fast.

4. Start confessing your sins and releasing forgiveness on all who have offended you. Shed weights of bitterness and reject the gall of iniquity.

5. Prepare yourself mentally for the fact that you are going to experience temporary pain which will lead to permanent gain.

6. Never forget that: There's no easy path to glory, there's no rosy road to fame; life, however, we may view it, is no simple parlor game; but its prizes call for fighting, for endurance and grit; for a rugged disposition.

Heb 12: 2: Jesus endured the cross because of the joy that was set before Him. Focus on the testimony and what you will gain if you complete this fast.

Your crown of glory awaits you!

PRAYER GUIDE

Gather your mind, soul and spirit. Don't allow your attention to be divided.

Make sure that you are at peace with God and everybody.

Before starting, sing two songs of mercy and three songs of worship.

While doing the 21 days **Power-Packed** miraculous prayers, hold this book on your left hand put your right hand up and start the prayers.

While doing the prayers or after it, perhaps you have attacks you are advised to keep on doing the prayer for more days; because victorious testimonies are coming your way, Amen.

Without faith you cannot please God; so, while doing this prayer for 21 days please try to develop a dynamic mountain-moving faith, that after doing this prayer the purpose of doing this prayer will be granted.

Start the prayer from **page 27** stop at **page 57**, and do it all at once...

Choose your **fasting plan** (see the table above) and complete it faithfully.

Also see the back **page 64** on a **guide to end FASTING and PRAYER.**

BEING READY FOR THE

BATTLE

NOW IS THE TIME FOR HOLY DISTURBANCE
Luke 18:1-7

AS YOU ARE GOING INTO THE 21 DAYS PRAYER IN THE NEXT CHAPTER BE DETERMINE TO:

- Create open heavens for the angels of your blessings.
- Paralyze angels that are contending with our angels of blessing.
- Break forte every bondage and barriers to your blessings

The Bible is abundant with instances of individuals persistently seeking God for their necessities. Unlike humans, God doesn't grow weary of persistent entreaties. Instead, He springs into action to assist you in your hour of need.

James 5:16: "The effectual fervent prayer of a righteous man availeth much."

The man who can pray has nothing to fear. The key that changes God's promises to reality is prayer. We are told to "pray without ceasing" (1 Thessalonians 5:17). And Isaiah says, "And give him no rest, till he establishes, and till he makes Jerusalem a praise in

27

the earth." (Isaiah 62:7). Perpetual prayer is essential, for there exist unseen powers determined to obstruct our supplications, as witnessed in the story of Daniel (*Daniel 10*). These adversaries engage in conflict against the very angels dispatched to deliver our answers. If you find yourself in a season where Heaven appears silent and your prayers seem to rebound from an impenetrable barrier, it becomes imperative to assertively break through the heavenly realm.

Our prayer has to be:

Effectual: They have to be able to produce the desired results; they have to be productive and fruitful.

Fervent: They have to be boiling, hot, warfare prayers said passionately from the heart. Violent. Strong.

In the realm of prayer, two crucial elements must be present. Prayer is a sacred act for those who walk in righteousness; a prayer offered by one steeped in sin is detestable in the eyes of the Lord. Holiness is an essential prerequisite for answered prayers. When prayer becomes fervent and potent, and the petitioner stands in righteousness, it serves as a conduit for supernatural and unparalleled breakthroughs to manifest in our lives!

Go into the prayer and have your victory.

Shalom!

THE BEGINNING

O GOD, I PRAISE AND THANK YOU

Start the prayer here from pages; all at once.

Everlasting and majestic God of heaven and earth, I lift my voice in exaltation and adoration to your glorious name. You alone are worthy of all praise and worship. I am filled with gratitude for the privilege to approach your presence and utter this prayer. As it is written, *"Oh, give thanks to the Lord, for He is good! For His mercy endures forever"* (*1 Chronicles 16:34*).

Oh God, the very breath I breathe is a testament to your unfailing grace. I offer you unending praise and thanksgiving in the mighty and miraculous name of Jesus. My heart overflows with gratitude because I know that you hold the power to answer prayers and perform astounding miracles. With unwavering faith, I declare that you will respond to my supplications in the most resounding manner, for your name is the epitome of divine responsiveness. Amen.

I extol and glorify you, O God of extraordinary testimonies. I am convinced that you delight in granting testimonies to those who earnestly seek you. Receive my fervent praise, for even as I start this prayer, I anticipate being enveloped in wondrous testimonies of your faithfulness and supernatural intervention. In the mighty and miraculous name of Jesus Christ of Nazareth.

(Here, sing any three songs of thanksgiving and praises to God)

MERCY OF THE ALMIGHTY GOD

Sing three songs of mercy here and read *2 Chronicles 7: 14-15* before praying this.

Notice: *If you really want to receive your miracle before you finish this prayer, kneel for about 15 minutes crying to God about your sinful life. Repent sincerely from all your sins and promise God that you will not return to them. Then open your Bible and pray Psalms 51 and 130.*

Merciful and forgiving God, I humbly come before you, seeking your boundless mercy and forgiveness. I acknowledge my shortcomings and transgressions, and I ask for your loving grace to cleanse me of all my sins. In your abundant mercy, wash away my iniquities and restore me to a place of righteousness. Lord, I repent and turn away from my sinful ways, seeking your guidance and strength to walk in your perfect will. Grant me a contrite heart and a spirit that seeks after you. May your merciful love envelop me and lead me on the path of righteousness. I trust in your unfailing mercy and forgiveness, knowing that you are faithful to forgive and restore. In Jesus' merciful name, I pray. Amen.

(Call the blood of Jesus Christ of Nazareth 7 times to cleanse your body, soul and spirit from all unrighteousness).

OPEN HEAVEN FOR AMAZING MIRACLES AND TESTIMONIES

O Mighty God, who answers prayers with signs and wonders, I stand in awe of your power and might. Your word declares, *"Call unto me, and I will answer thee and show thee great and mighty things which thou knowest not" (Jeremiah 33:3)*. In the name of Jesus Christ of Nazareth, I boldly call upon your name, knowing that you are faithful to your promises. As I embark on this 21-day prayer journey, I declare that your heaven is open above me, and your divine favor surrounds me.

You, God of covenant and promise, I remind you of your word that says, *"When God made a promise to Abraham because he could swear by no greater, he swore by himself" (Hebrews 6:13)*. I hold onto your faithful promises, and I believe that as I pray in the power of the Holy Spirit, miracles will manifest in my life. Let the miraculous be my portion in these 21 days of fervent prayer.

With unwavering faith, I anticipate your amazing answers to my prayers. All glory and honor belong to you, Almighty God. In the mighty and miraculous name of Jesus Christ, I pray. Amen.

(For about 10 minutes, kneel and pray very well to God that you want him to bless you with amazing miracles and testimonies all through the duration of this prayer.)

MIRACULOUS SIGNS AND WONDERS IN THE BLOOD OF JESUS CHRIST

Almighty Father, God of heaven, I approach your throne with boldness, where the precious blood of Jesus Christ is available. My God and Lord, let your miraculous signs and wonders be unleashed upon me in this very moment of prayer. May my life be transformed by the supernatural power of the Holy Ghost, in the mighty name of Jesus Christ of Nazareth.

I invoke the miraculous blood of Jesus Christ to flow through every aspect of my being, my family, and my business. Let the signs and wonders in the blood demolish every stronghold of evil that has been programmed against me. By the power of the Holy Spirit, I declare victory in the mighty name of Jesus Christ of Nazareth. Amen.

(Say the prayer here seven times with authority).

Through the miraculous blood of Jesus Christ, I command every attacking situation that hinders my progress to vanish, dissolve, and be destroyed by the power of the Holy Spirit. Amen. In the mighty name of Jesus of Nazareth, I declare divine intervention and breakthrough, ushering in a season of testimonies and victory. Amen.

Let the glorious blood of Jesus bring forth a miraculous transformation in my life. Amen.

(Say the prayer here 2 times with a believing faith that it has happened.)

Almighty God of heaven your word says *"And they overcome him by the blood of the lamb ... " (Rev. 12:11).* Through the power of the Holy Spirit, I overcome by the blood of the lamb of God Jesus Christ all evil power and situation fighting to overcome me, go and disappear out of my life and come back no more in Jesus miraculous name, Amen.

Let every attacking situation standing in my way vanish through the power of the Holy Spirit in the mighty name of Jesus. Nazareth, Amen.

GOD, RELEASE YOUR MIRACULOUS ANGELS

Almighty, glorious and powerful God, your greatness is so real and you are truly powerful. For your word says, "And, lo. the angel of the Lord came upon them

and the glory of the Lord shone round about them ... "
(Luke 2:9).

"And of the angels he saith, Who maketh his angels'
spirits .... " (Heb. 1:7).

Glorious and mighty God, I beseech you to release
your ministering spirit and powerful angels into this
sacred space where I lift my prayer. Let your radiant
and miraculous presence envelop me, igniting divine
transformation and breakthroughs in my life and
business. May the manifestation of great miracles be
evident as I fervently seek you, O Lord, in the mighty
and wondrous name of Jesus Christ of Nazareth,
Amen. With gratitude in my heart, I acknowledge the
workings of your mighty ministering angels in every
aspect of my life, and I celebrate the testimonies that
shall unfold, magnifying your name. Amen.

Holy Spirit, Divine Comforter, we recognize
that it is through Your presence that we find
solace, guidance, and strength. We open our
hearts wide, ready to receive Your
transformative power and the gifts You bring.
Flow through our lives like a gentle breeze,
sweeping away all that hinders our connection
with You.

Touch our minds, O Holy Spirit, and illuminate
the corridors of our thoughts with Your divine
wisdom. Grant us clarity of purpose, that we
may discern Your will for our lives and follow it
faithfully. Help us to align our desires and

aspirations with the path You have set before us, that we may walk in harmony with Your divine plan.

Infuse our hearts, O Holy Spirit, with Your all-encompassing love. Pour Your healing balm upon the wounds we carry, soothing our pain and bringing forth forgiveness and reconciliation. Teach us to love unconditionally, as You have loved us, that our lives may become a reflection of Your divine compassion.

ANOINT MY TONGUE

In the mighty name of Jesus, I fervently pray, O heavenly Father, that you fill me with the overflowing power and authority of your Holy Spirit. Let my tongue be anointed as a mighty flame of fire, releasing words of life and transformation. As your Word declares, *"Death and life are in the power of the tongue, and those who love it will eat its fruit" (Proverbs 18:21)*. Sovereign God, you hold all power and might in your hands.

Heavenly Father, I beseech you to anoint my lips with the fire of your Holy Spirit, that in this sacred hour, each uttered prayer shall carry the weight of your prophetic power.

Let your divine will be established and fulfilled through these sacred petitions, as we claim the authority granted to us in the mighty name of Jesus.

Oh, let the heavens bear witness as these fervent petitions reverberate through the realms of eternity, stirring mighty angels to action and unveiling your glory upon the earth. May the resonance of our faith move mountains, break chains, and bring divine transformations as we declare in Jesus mighty name.

May these words of us resound in the realms of the supernatural, bringing forth manifestations that align with your perfect plan. Amen

In faith, we declare it done, knowing that our prayers shall find favor and victory in the glorious name of Jesus. Amen and amen.

DECLARING WAR DISASTER

In the mighty and matchless name of Jesus, I come before you, Heavenly Father, with unwavering faith, knowing that you have anointed my tongue with divine power and authority. With this authority, I boldly decree and declare warfare and confusion within the Kingdom of Satan and his agents where my name has been registered. I shatter every bondage that the enemy has imposed on me, and I nullify every record bearing my name in their domain. Your Word proclaims, *"You will also decree a thing, and it will be established for you; and light will shine on your ways" (Job 22:28).*

In the majestic name of Jesus, I unleash the warfare of confusion upon the kingdom of darkness, frustrating their prayers and thwarting their attacks on every area of my life—my business, work, education, future, and my being. As your Word declares, *"The adversaries of the Lord shall be broken to pieces; from heaven He will thunder against them" (1 Samuel 2:10).*

Therefore, in the name of Jesus, I release the thunderous power of God from heaven to dismantle every instrument that Satan and his agents have employed to shield themselves. Let their influence be eradicated from every part of my property. Furthermore, I command the fire of the Holy Spirit to consume and destroy every spiritual device used to monitor me. In Jesus' mighty name, amen.

(Please pray Psalm 35 now)

MADE COVENANT

Heavenly Father, I approach your throne of grace in the mighty and exalted name of your Son, Jesus Christ. I boldly exercise the authority and power bestowed upon me by you to shatter every covenant I have knowingly or unknowingly made with Satan and his agents. I declare the annulment of every agreement made by my ancestors on my behalf, breaking their influence over my life, in the matchless name of Jesus Christ. Your word assures me, *"Your covenant with death shall be disannulled, and your agreement with hell shall not stand; when the overflowing scourge passes through, you will be trampled down by it" (Isaiah 28:19)*.

By the anointing and power of the Holy Spirit, I declare that all these covenants are now rendered null and void in the name of Jesus. I am released from their grip, and their effects are abolished in every area of my life. I stand in the freedom and authority granted to me by the precious blood of Jesus. In the victorious name of Jesus Christ, I proclaim this truth, believing that every chain is broken and I am set free. Amen and amen.

HOLDING BOUND ALL ANTI-PRAYER EVIL POWERS

Mighty and awe-inspiring God, I exalt and magnify your name in the mighty and majestic name of Jesus Christ, Amen. Father, your word reveals the battles fought in the heavenly realms, as depicted in *Daniel 10:13*: *"But the prince of the kingdom of Persia withstood me twenty-one days; and behold, Michael, one of the chief princes, came to help me, for I had been left alone there with the kings of Persia."*

Glorious God, through the power of your Holy Spirit, I boldly decree and declare spiritual warfare against every kingdom of Satan and his agents that seek to hinder and obstruct the fulfillment of my prayers. I command every spirit of delay and obstruction to be expelled and cast out in the mighty and triumphant name of Jesus Christ of Nazareth, Amen.

By the authority vested in me through Christ, I proclaim victory and breakthrough over every spiritual opposition that seeks to prevent the manifestation of answered prayers. I declare that my prayers shall prevail, and the forces of darkness shall be rendered powerless. In the name of Jesus, I stand firm and resolute, trusting in your mighty power to overcome all obstacles. Amen and amen.

(Say the prayer here 7 times with boiling anger and authority)

By the anointing power of the Holy Spirit, I release thunder, lightning, and fire to scatter every dark cloud and opposing forces that wage war against my prayers in the mighty and triumphant name of Jesus Christ of Nazareth, Amen.

Through the anointing power of the Holy Spirit, I decree that every weakness, distraction, and deviation from the path of prayer shall vanish in the victorious and all-powerful name of Jesus Christ of Nazareth, Amen.

O Almighty God, the Father of miraculous answers, dispatch your heavenly angels to swiftly bring forth the answers and manifestations to my prayers in the mighty and responsive name of Jesus Christ, Amen.

Let every prince of Persia withholding my prayers, my breakthroughs, my finances, my marriage, my academics, my upliftment and divine elevation receive thunder of God and die by fire in the mighty name of Jesus Christ.

REJECT AND RENOUNCE

In the mighty name of Jesus Christ, I stand against you, Satan, and your agents. I obliterate and renounce all your projections, manipulations, spiritual mirrors, and every instrument of darkness used against me. They are destroyed and rejected in Jesus' name.

(Say the prayer here 3 times)

Because the word of God says *"for the weapon of our warfare are not Carnal but mighty through God to the pulling down of strongholds, casting down imaginations and every high thing that exalteth itself against the knowledge of God and brings into captivity every thought to the obedience of Christ "(2 Corinthians 4.5).*

By the divine authority bestowed upon me through the word of God, I declare the destruction and dismantling of every stronghold erected by Satan. In the name of Jesus, I abolish and uproot every demonic influence present in my family, business, body, soul, and spirit.

Their powers are cast into the bottomless pit, never to rise against me again. Amen.

With the power of the Holy Spirit and the heavenly angels, I enter your domain, O kingdom of darkness, and I set myself free. My soul, spirit, body, business, family, and possessions are liberated by the mighty name of Jesus. For it is written, *"The Son of God appeared for this purpose, to destroy the works of the devil"* *(1 John 3:8)*.

(Say this prayer here 3 times)

In the mighty and all-conquering name of Jesus Christ, I declare the total annihilation of every work of the devil in my life. Sickness, poverty, failure, disappointment, curses, and barrenness, I cast you out by the authority vested in me through Jesus Christ. By the power of His precious blood, I reject and renounce all possessions of Satan that have infiltrated my life.

In the victorious name of Jesus, I decree divine healing and restoration upon my soul, body, spirit, family, and business. The Word of God declares that Jesus Himself carried our infirmities and bore our sicknesses. By His stripes, we are healed. I proclaim this truth three times, affirming my faith in His miraculous healing power.

By the consuming fire of the Holy Spirit, I come against every demonic force that torments and terrifies me in my dreams. I bind you in the name of Jesus. For the Word in Psalms says, *"Behold, I have given you authority to tread on serpents and scorpions and over all the power of the enemy, and nothing shall hurt you."*

I stand firm in the authority and power of Jesus Christ, confident that every demonic force is defeated, every work of the devil is destroyed, and I am victorious in Him. Amen and amen!

"Whatsoever ye shall bind on earth shall be bound in heaven and whatsoever ye shall loose on earth shall be loosed in heaven" (Matt 18: 18),

I exercise the authority and power of the highest God over you in Jesus' name. You demons of bad dreams, I come against you and cancel all of the bad dreams I have had in my life.

I reject and renounce all of them because God has given me the authority to lose and bind all the powers of the devil.

Therefore, **I lose myself from every hold of the enemy and cast the demons into the bottomless pit in Jesus' name, Amen.**

GARMENTS OF UNRIGHTEOUSNESS STANDING AGAINST ME

God of great mercy and compassion look upon me with your unfailing love and have mercy on me in these 21 days prayer that I am doing, in the mighty name of Jesus Christ, Amen. For your word says: *"Joshua was standing there wearing filthy clothes. The angel said to his heavenly attendants, take away the filthy clothes this man is wearing. Then he said to Joshua, I have taken away your sin and will give you new clothes to wear" - (Zech. 3:3).*

Oh, God of immense and boundless love, let your divine work in the life of Joshua be replicated in my own life. Strip away every filthy garment that stands as a hindrance against me, and cleanse me from all my sins through the powerful and responsive name of Jesus Christ of Nazareth. Amen.

Mighty God, just as you dispatched your angel to rebuke Satan when he dared to accuse Joshua in your holy presence, I implore you to send forth your heavenly messengers to rebuke every satanic force and demonic accusation that stands in opposition to my blessings and breakthroughs in this prayer. Let them be banished, scattered, and utterly defeated by the unstoppable power of the Holy Spirit. In the mighty and miraculous name of Jesus Christ of Nazareth, let my garments of unrighteousness be completely destroyed. Amen. Oh, God, adorn me with the righteous garment that enables me to receive abundantly from you. Clothe me with divine favor, blessings, and open doors in the mighty and responsive name of Jesus Christ of Nazareth. Amen

ATTACKERS OF MY DESTINY AND PLANS, GO BY FIRE AND THUNDER

Oh, Almighty and all-powerful God, I come before Your divine presence, fully aware of the attacks against my destiny and plans. As I stand in faith, I declare that Your Word shall manifest in my life.

In the name of Jesus Christ of Nazareth, I invoke the power of Your Holy Spirit to arise with fiery indignation and thunderous might against every force that seeks to hinder my purpose and destiny. Let the enemies of my progress be scattered, shattered, and utterly destroyed by the consuming fire of Your divine presence.

I command every evil attacker, whether through sickness, affliction, or any form of hindrance, to be consumed by the rain of fire and thunder from heaven. Let the chains that bind me be shattered, and let every padlock hindering my breakthrough be utterly demolished by the glorious power of the Holy Spirit.

By the authority vested in me through Jesus Christ, I declare that every evil force opposing my destiny shall be crushed and obliterated. I decree their defeat and expulsion from my life, never to return, as Your divine fire and thunder reign supreme. Amen.

No longer shall the attackers of my destiny have any hold over me. By the power of Your mighty hand, I am set free and propelled towards the fulfillment of my divine purpose. I walk in victory and triumph, knowing that You are fighting on my behalf. Amen.

In the name of Jesus Christ of Nazareth, I seal this prayer with the certainty that every evil attacker has been vanquished. I give You all the glory, honor, and praise, for You alone are worthy. Amen and amen.

TOTAL DELIVERANCE

(Please pray *Psalm 71, 35 & 60* now)

Almighty Father, in the mighty and prophetic name of Jesus Christ, I stand before you in this sacred place of total deliverance. As I pray, I invoke the power of *Psalm 71, 35,* and *60,* aligning myself with your divine Word.

I boldly declare that this place is transformed into Mount Zion, were healing and deliverance flow abundantly. I reject and break every spell, projection, charm, enchantment, divination, or concoction that has been aimed at my body, soul, spirit, and possessions. Your Word assures me that *"no enchantment can prevail against Jacob, and no divination against Israel" (Numbers 23:23).*

The 21 Days Powerful Miraculous Prayer

In the name of Jesus Christ, I liberate myself and all that pertains to me from the bondage of occultic and satanic kingdoms. I claim the fulfillment of the scripture that says, *"Lose him and let him go"* *(John 11:47)*. By the anointing power of the Holy Spirit, I declare that every burden, yoke, and evil power upon my life is shattered and destroyed.

I repeat this prayer three times, reinforcing the declaration of my freedom from the clutches of Satan and his forces. Your Word assures me that *"if the Son (Jesus Christ) sets you free, you will be free indeed"* *(John 8:36)*. Therefore, I proclaim with confidence that I am free from every power of darkness.

Lord Jesus Christ, I wholeheartedly believe that through the power of your Spirit, you have set me free today. I thank you for your faithfulness and deliverance in my life. May your name be glorified forever and ever. Amen.

"Surely, he shall deliver thee from the snare of the fowler and from the noisome pestilence" - Psalm 91:3

"Thou hast turned for me my mourning into dancing: thou hast put off my sackcloth, and girded me with gladness" - Psalm 30:11

"The Spirit of the Lord is upon me because he hath anointed me to preach the gospel to the poor; he hath sent me to heal the brokenhearted, to preach deliverance to the captives, and recovering of sight to the blind, to set at liberty them that are bruised" - Luke 4:18

MIRACULOUSLY INTERVENE, O GOD AND REMOVE EVERY STUBBORN PROBLEM FROM ME

O Miraculous and powerful God of mercy and compassion, I humbly come before you, knowing that you are the One who can intervene in the midst of my sleepless nights caused by these overwhelming problems. I firmly believe that through this heartfelt prayer, you will extend your helping hand and deliver me from these challenges in the mighty and miraculous name of Jesus Christ. Amen.

"For nothing is impossible with God." - Luke 1:37

In the mighty name of Jesus Christ of Nazareth, I boldly command every mountain of stubborn problems in my life to be uprooted and utterly destroyed by the anointing power of the Holy Ghost. No obstacle or hindrance shall stand against the authority of the name of Jesus. Through the glorious anointing power of the Holy Ghost, I demolish every scheme and plot of the evil one designed to bring disgrace and shame upon my physical or spiritual life. I nullify and obliterate every problem programmed to rob me of abundant life and I emerge victorious over them all in the mighty and triumphant name of Jesus Christ of Nazareth. Amen.

The 21 Days Powerful Miraculous Prayer

For I know *"No weapon forged against you will prevail, and you will refute every tongue that accuses you. This is the heritage of the servants of the LORD, and this is their vindication from me," declares the LORD". - Isaiah 54:17*

God of mercy, I fervently beseech you to supernaturally intervene in these problems, so that at the end of this prayer, I will have a powerful testimony of the great things you have done for me. You are the God who turns impossible situations into glorious outcomes. Thank you, Heavenly Father, for your faithfulness in answering my prayer and bringing forth miraculous solutions. May all glory and honor be unto you *"..who is able to do immeasurably more than all we ask or imagine, according to his power that is at work within us." - Ephesians 3:20*

"The LORD is my rock, my fortress, and my deliverer; my God is my rock, in whom I take refuge, my shield and the horn of my salvation, my stronghold." - Psalm 18:2

Heavenly Father, in your infinite mercy and compassion, I place my trust in your unfailing love and unfathomable power. I know that you are the one who can bring about miraculous interventions and deliverance. I eagerly anticipate the day when I will testify of the mighty works you have performed in my life. I declare that you are faithful to your promises, and I thank you in advance for the manifestation of your greatness. May your name be glorified, now and forever. Amen.

TOTAL RESTORATION

Heavenly Father, I come before you with a heart filled with gratitude for all that you have done in my life. I thank you specifically for the privilege of approaching you in prayer through the name of your beloved Son, Jesus Christ, who sacrificed himself on the cross to deliver me from the clutches of darkness.

Lord God, I beseech you to restore everything that the enemy has stolen from me. In the powerful and mighty name of Jesus, I declare restoration over every area of my life. Amen.

I pray, O God, that you grant me the power of restoration. By the authority bestowed upon me through the Holy Spirit, I proclaim that when I speak forth restoration, it shall manifest in glorious abundance. In the name of Jesus Christ, may your restoration power be activated and realized. Amen.

Your word declares, *"The thief comes only to steal, kill, and destroy; but I have come that they may have life, and have it abundantly"* (John 10:10). Furthermore, your word assures us, *"But if he is found, he must restore sevenfold; he must give up all the substance of his house"* (Proverbs 6:31).

Therefore, I fervently pray, Lord, restore everything the enemy has stolen from me. In the mighty name of Jesus, I call forth a sevenfold restoration over every aspect of my life, my business, my body, my soul, my spirit, my family, and all my endeavors.

I command you, demonic forces of infirmity, poverty, disappointment, failure, sickness, curses, backwardness, unfruitfulness, and sleepless nights, to restore all that you have taken from me, sevenfold, in the name of Jesus Christ.

For you have declared in *Joel 2:25*, *"I will restore to you the years that the swarming locust has eaten, the crawling locust, the consuming locust, and the chewing locust."*

Lord, I thank you for the promises in your word. I pray that through the anointing power of the Holy Spirit, everything that Satan and his agents have stolen from me will be restored sevenfold. According to your word, let restoration manifest in my life, in the mighty name of Jesus. Amen.

GOD'S MIRACULOUS HEALING POWER

(This prayer here is for only those that reed God's healing miracle)

(Before you start the prayer here, open your Bible now and pray Psalms 57 and 41).

Start:

Almighty God, the sovereign ruler of Heaven and Earth, I come before you with unwavering faith in your mighty healing power. I beseech you to manifest your glorious power within me as I pray, that I may experience the miraculous touch of your Holy Spirit, bringing forth divine healing in every aspect of my being. In the mighty and matchless name of Jesus, I pray. Amen.

O God, I hold fast to your eternal word which declares, *"Forever, O Lord, your word is settled in heaven" (Psalm 119:89)*, and *"For with God nothing shall be impossible" (Luke 1:37)*. By the authority of your settled word and the power that makes the impossible possible, I declare that every bondage of sickness that holds me captive in my body, soul, spirit, blood, bones, and veins shall be utterly destroyed by the consuming fire of the Holy Spirit and the cleansing power of the precious blood of Jesus Christ. Amen.

I decree and declare that every form of sickness that entered me through sin, ancestral lineage, manipulations of evil powers, or any hidden sickness shall be washed away and expelled miraculously from my being. Through the anointing power of the Holy Spirit and the miraculous blood of Jesus Christ, I command them to be eradicated completely in the mighty and miraculous name of Jesus Christ. Amen.

I invite the miraculous healing water from the wounds of Jesus Christ of Nazareth to enter into me and bring forth healing from all forms of disease and sickness. Let your healing flow through every fiber of my being, restoring me to complete health and wholeness. Amen.

I also invoke the miraculous healing power of the blood that flowed from the head and stripes of Jesus

Christ of Nazareth. Let this sacred blood heal me from every ailment and affliction in my body, soul, and spirit. By the power of the Holy Spirit, I receive divine healing, restoration, and renewal in the name of Jesus Christ of Nazareth. Amen.

MIRACULOUS BUSINESS BREAKTHROUGH

Almighty God of great power and might, your word says: "...I will lose the lions of kings, to open before him the two leaved gates and the gates shall not be shut: I will go before thee and make the crooked places straight, I will break in pieces the gates of brass, and cut in sunder the bars of iron and I will give thee the treasures of darkness, and hidden riches of secret places, that thou mayest know that I the Lord, which call thee by thy name, am the God of Israel " (Isaiah 45:1-3).

Mighty and All-Powerful God, by the unfathomable power of Your Holy Spirit, I decree that any plots, attacks, failures, disappointments, backwardness, and diversions orchestrated by evil forces against me shall crumble into dust. Every business problem, instability, financial lack, and chains used to bind my business shall be consumed by the fire and thunder of Your divine wrath in the miraculous name of Jesus Christ. Amen.

I beseech You, O God of war, to arise and scatter the plans of the enemy. Let every charm, key, and chain used to lock up my business be shattered into irreparable pieces. Open the floodgates of miraculous breakthrough, granting me access to hidden riches, the treasures of darkness, and abundant divine provisions for every aspect of my business. May my business experience limitless growth, both financially and in all other realms, by the mighty name of Jesus Christ of Nazareth. Amen.

O Mighty God, just as You blessed Job and granted him a miraculous breakthrough, I humbly come before You, seeking the same favor. By the power of the Holy Spirit, I decree and declare that from this moment forward, every aspect of my life shall experience unprecedented success and progress in Jesus' name. amen.

In the mighty and miraculous name of Jesus Christ of Nazareth, I invoke the anointing power of the Holy Spirit and the cleansing power of the blood of Jesus to nullify every evil money operating within my business. Let these wicked schemes aimed at causing harm and hindrance be turned back upon the senders with swift and powerful force, consumed by fire and thunder by the power of the holy spirit in Jesus' mighty name.

I stand firm in faith, knowing that Your divine intervention is at work. Grant me the breakthrough and favor that will surpass all human understanding. May my path be illuminated with divine guidance, leading me to extraordinary success and blessings in every endeavor. amen

In the name of Jesus Christ, I decree and receive this miraculous breakthrough, trusting in Your unfailing love and infinite power. Amen and amen!

God Almighty, your word is powerful on every kind of sickness. Your word says: *"He (Lord) sent his word and healed them and delivered them from their destructions" (Psalm 107:20).* Powerful God that heals without limit, you miraculously healed a man who was ill for 38 years in *John 5:58.* You went about miraculously healing all manner of diseases in *Acts 10:38.* You are still the same, come and miraculously heal me. You are the only one that can help me as I am saying this prayer through the miraculous healing power in the name of Jesus Christ of Nazareth, Amen.

MIRACULOUS OPEN DOORS FOR FAVOUR AND BLESSINGS

O Mighty God, my Lord and Redeemer, I call upon your divine presence to arise in your unmatched power and radiant glory. As I, with unwavering faith, declare that every evil force and dark power hindering my open doors, favor, and blessings shall be confronted by the consuming fire of the holy ghost. amen

In the majestic name of Jesus Christ of Nazareth, I command your mighty power of destruction to overtake and overthrow every opposing force that seeks to hinder my progress. Let them be utterly vanquished, dismantled, and rendered powerless in the mighty name of Jesus Christ. Amen.

I speak with authority and conviction, knowing that no weapon formed against me shall prosper. By the power of the living God, I proclaim deliverance from all forces of darkness that dare to stand in my way in the mighty name of Jesus Christ of Nazareth. amen

God, Your word says: *"Thou shalt arise, and have mercy upon Zion for the time to favor her yea, the set time has come" (Psalm 105:187)*. My God, let the atmosphere shift, and let your divine favor flow abundantly in every area of my life. May your blessings cascade upon me like a mighty river, as I walk in alignment with your will.

"For thou Lord, wilt blesses the righteous; with favour will thou compass him as with a shield" (Psalm 3:12).

I declare this prayer in faith, knowing that you are the God who performs miracles and makes the impossible possible. I trust in your unfailing love and your unwavering faithfulness to bring about the breakthroughs in Jesus' name. amen

In the name of Jesus, I claim victory over every obstacle, every hindrance, and every evil power that seeks to hinder my progress. I stand boldly in the authority bestowed upon me as a child of the Most High God to declare open doors in Jesus name. amen.

My God, I thank you in advance for the great and miraculous victory that is already unfolding. I praise your holy name and give you all the glory, for you alone are worthy.

Amen and amen!

PROTECTION POWER OF GOD

Father God of heaven, I thank you because you are the God who comes to help and protect your people.

Your word says: *"For He (God) shall give his angels charge over you (Me) to keep thee (Me) in all thy ways" (Psalm 91:11)*.

And your word says again: *"The angel of the Lord encampeth round about them, that fear him and delivereth them." (Psalm 34:7)*.

Lord Jesus, in the mighty and powerful name of Jesus Christ, I fervently pray for the divine intervention of Your heavenly host. I beseech You to dispatch Your mighty angels to encamp around me, covering me and everything that belongs to me with the overflowing and triumphant blood of Jesus Christ.

Father, I humbly implore You to shield me from the relentless attacks of the devil and his agents. Whenever they gather against me, I decree and declare in the name of Jesus that they shall be scattered like chaff before the wind. Your word assures me, saying, *"Behold, they shall surely gather together, but not by Me. Whosoever shall* gather against you shall fall for your sake" *(Isaiah 54:15)*.

By the authority bestowed upon me as a child of God, I command that whenever Satan and his agents plot against me and my family, their kingdom shall be thrown into utter confusion in the name of Jesus. For Your word proclaims, *"When the enemy shall come in like a flood, the Spirit of the Lord shall lift up a standard against him" (Isaiah 59:19)*.

Heavenly Father, In the face of adversity and the encroachment of the enemy, we declare Your mighty promise from Isaiah 59:19:

With unwavering faith, we boldly proclaim that Your Spirit is our impenetrable fortress. It rises as an unyielding standard against every form of opposition, evil, or harm that dares to approach us.

We stand firmly on Your Word, declaring that no weapon formed against us shall prosper, and every tongue that rises against us in judgment shall be utterly defeated (Isaiah 54:17).

Lord, Your Spirit is our refuge, our strength, and our shield in times of trouble. We speak this truth into our lives, trusting that Your divine protection surrounds us at all times.

In the powerful name of Jesus Christ, our Savior and Redeemer, we make this declaration.

Amen and amen.

DECLARATION

In the name of our Heavenly Father and Creator, I stand with the authority vested in me through our Lord and Savior, Jesus Christ. I boldly declare that every force of darkness, every principality, and every power that dares to oppose me/us shall crumble and be rendered powerless.

I decree and declare with unwavering faith that affliction, in any form, shall not dare to rise again in our lives. I proclaim this with divine assurance, firmly rooted in the mighty and most gracious name of Jesus Christ of Nazareth.

Amen, and so it is, for His glory and our victory.

THANKSGIVING

Gracious Father, with hearts overflowing in gratitude, as we have poured our heart to You, acknowledging Your divine presence and Your unwavering love. We thank You for hearing our prayers and answering them according to Your perfect will.

Lord, we are humbled by Your grace and mercy. I offer profound gratitude for hearing and answering every petition we've brought before Your throne, You have answered with wisdom and love through the powerful name of Jesus Christ, Your beloved Son.

May all glory, honor, adoration, and praise be eternally ascribed to You alone, now and forevermore. Amen.

My Maker, You are the giver of all good gifts, as we lift our voices in thanksgiving, we declare that Your faithfulness knows no bounds. You have guided us, protected us, and provided for us in ways that are beyond our understanding. Your love has illuminated our lives, and Your blessings have filled our hearts.

We thank You for the answered prayers, both great and small, and for the miracles You have bestowed upon us. May our lives be a testament to Your glory and Your love.

In the name of Jesus Christ, our Savior and Redeemer, we offer this prayer of thanksgiving.

Amen and amen.

Share The Grace

(Please pray this Psalms, 23, 91 now), and sing three songs of thanks to God.

See page 46 for guide on breaking fasting

After Close The Prayer.

Grateful Hearts: Praying, Trusting, and Receiving Through Jesus Christ

Dear Beloved,

In our journey of faith, gratitude is the radiant thread that weaves our prayers, trust, and reception of divine blessings through Jesus Christ. It is a powerful force that opens the gates of heaven, allowing the abundance of God's grace to pour into our lives.

Praying with Gratitude

Philippians 4:6 reminds us, "Do not be anxious about anything, but in every situation, by prayer and petition, with thanksgiving, present your requests to God." When we approach our Creator in prayer with hearts full of gratitude, we acknowledge His goodness and mercy. Gratitude transforms our petitions into sweet conversations with our Heavenly Father.

Trusting with Gratitude

Proverbs 3:5-6 assures us, "Trust in the Lord with all your heart and lean not on your own understanding; in all your ways submit to him, and he will make your paths straight." As we trust in Jesus Christ, our Savior, we do so with thanksgiving for His sacrificial love and unwavering presence. Gratitude deepens our faith and allows us to lean into His divine wisdom.

The 21 Days Powerful Miraculous Prayer

Receiving with Gratitude

James 1:17 reminds us, "Every good and perfect gift is from above, coming down from the Father of the heavenly lights." When we receive blessings through Jesus Christ, our hearts overflow with gratitude. Gratitude acknowledges that every blessing is a gift, undeserved and given out of God's boundless love.

Living a Grateful Life

Gratitude extends beyond prayer; it becomes a way of life. *1 Thessalonians 5:18* instructs us, "Give thanks in all circumstances; for this is God's will for you in Christ Jesus." In every season, whether of abundance or trial, we remain grateful, for we trust that God is working all things together for our good *(Romans 8:28)*.

The Miracle of Gratitude

As we cultivate gratitude in our prayers, trust, and reception of blessings through Jesus Christ, we witness a miraculous transformation. Our hearts become more attuned to the presence of God. We find peace in His promises, strength in His grace, and joy in His love.

May gratitude be the melody of your prayer, the foundation of your trust, and the hallmark of your reception of blessings through Jesus Christ. Let it be the lens through which you see the beauty in every moment and the reminder of God's immeasurable goodness.

UNFAILING PROMISES OF GOD

WHERE TO FIND HELP IN TIME OF NEED

WHEN SEEKING THE FACE OF GOD:

Psalm 27:8; Psalm 105:4; 2 Chronicles 7:14; Hebrews 11:6

FOR DIVINE INTERVENTION

Jeremiah 33:3; Matthew 7:7-8

FOR SECURITY AND PROTECTION:

Job 5:26; Psalm 128: 6; Deut 33:27; Psalm. 127:1-2; Isaiah 4:5; Psalm. 7:8-9; Ps. 50:15; Ps. 27; Luke 10:19; Ps. 91; Colossians 3:3; Isaiah 54:15; 17; Ps. 121: 3-4; 2 Kings 6:13-17; ZECH 2:5, 8; Dan. 3:27; 2 Chron 16:9.

WHEN DISCOURAGED, MEDITATE ON:

Ps. 27:14; 37:7; 42; 43; Isaiah 3: 10; 40:1-5; Isaiah 41:10; Jer 32:17; 32:27

WHEN DEPRESSED AND ANXIOUS:

Philippians 4:6; Matthew 6:25-31; 11:28; Ps. 34; 42; 46:10-11; 121, Isaiah 43:1-4; 26:3; John 14:1; Ps. 30:5.

FOR LONG LIFE:

EX. 23:26; Ps. 23:4; 90:10; 91:15-16; 128; Isaiah 46:3-5.

The 21 Days Powerful Miraculous Prayer

FOR THOSE PREGNANT:

1 Timothy 2:15; Exodus 1:19; 23:25-26; Job 21: 10.

FOR HEALING IN TIMES OF SICKNESS:

Ps. 6:2; 107:20; 103:3; 47:3; Isaiah 53:4; Exodus 15:26; 1 Peter 2:24.

FOR STABLE MARRIAGE:

Isaiah 3:10; Proverb 31:10-29; Ps. 1:3; Ps. 128; Ephesians 5:22-33. Ps. 68:6.

WHEN WAITING FOR AND EXPECTING A MIRACLE:

e.g. pregnancy, life-partner, job, academics.

Jeremiah 32:17; 32:27; Isaiah 49:23; Luke 1:37, Isaiah 41:10; 43:1-4; Ps. 30:5; Ps. 27:14; 37:7.

DELIVERANCE FROM ENEMIES:

Deut 33:27; Ps. 27; Ps. 23; Ps. 35; Isaiah 43:1-3; 44:25; 54:15, 17; 59:19; 1 John 4:4; 2 Kings 6:13-17.

FOR FAVOUR, MEDITATE ON:

Gen 39:1-5; Prov 3:1-4; 16:7; Isaiah 60:1-7; Ps. 5:11-12; Esther 5: 2-3; Ps 30:5; GENESIS 25:23; 48:19.

WHEN LONELY:

Deut 31:6; Ps. 23; Ps. 27; Hebrews 13:5; Matt 28:20.

FOR COURAGE AND BOLDNESS (WHEN AFRAID):

Deut 33:27; Joshua 1:3-7; Ps. 126; Hebrews 11; James 1:6-9; Ps.34; Ps. 23:4; Deut 31:6; Isaiah 41:10; Luke 10:19; 1 John 4:4

FOR GUIDANCE:

Isaiah 30:21; Ps. 23:2; Ps.32:8; Ps.40; John 14:14

FOR FRUIT OF THE WOMB:

Isaiah 54:1-8; Ps. 127:3-4; Exodus 23:26; Luke1:3

WHEN IN TROUBLE:

Deut. 33:27; Ps. 121; Isaiah 26:3; 43:1-4, 29; 44:25; 45:2-3; Luke 1:37; Ps. 23:4-6; John 14:1-4; Hebrews 7:25; Ps. 30:5; Isaiah 41:10

BEFORE TRAVELLING:

Ps. 121; 128; 91; Isaiah 54:17; Ps. 91:1

FOR STUDENTS (SUCCESS AND EXCELLENCE IN ACADEMICS AND EXAMS):

Gen 39:1-5; Ps. 119:34-125; Ps. 71:1-7, Daniel 1:10; Ecclesiastic 7:11-12

WHEN YOU NEED PROMOTION:

Psalm 75:6-7; Psalm 84:7

FOR REVIVAL FIRE/FRESH OIL

Rev 3:14-16; Ps. 138:6-8; 71:20; Hosea 6:1-3; Acts 2; John 7: 37-38; 1 Cor 14:15

IF YOU ARE A WIDOW/WIDOWER/ORPHAN:

Ps. 146:9; Job 29:12; Ps. 68:5

The 21 Days Powerful Miraculous Prayer

STARTING A BUSINESS:

Gen 39:1-5; Ps. 1:3; Ps. 90:16-17; Job 14:7; Deuteronomy 28:7-8; 11

WHEN YOU LACK MONEY/THINGS:

Job 36:11; Ps. 34:10; Matthew 6:33; Phil. 4:15; 3 John 2; John14:14; ISAIAH 41:18

WHEN IN CAPTIVE:

Psalm 34:17-18; Isaiah 61:1; 2 Corinthians 10:4

WHEN YOU ARE OPRESSED:

Isaiah 49:24-26; Psalm 9:9-10; Isaiah 41:10

PROCEDURE FOR BREAKING YOUR FAST

Believe that you have received all that you prayed for in this prayer and fasting program. Every obstacles set against your life/ministry shall bow and die in disgrace this year!

You can repeat the prayer points in this booklet once a month, especially at the beginning of each quarter throughout the year! Use the Unfailing God's Promises pages at the back too.

With your eye of faith, begin to see your answer (performance) in advance. The just shall live by faith. Until you see it, you cannot seize (hold) it. Live in thanksgiving and praise. Refuse to complain or murmur!

Wait for your season. There is a time to make things happen and a time to allow things to happen. Wait on God! Wait for your God-ordained season. Refuse to doubt God!

Break your fast with fruits and light food. This is to avoid abdominal cramps! Your body will not respond quickly to food. It is normal. Eat heavy food gradually. Watch and pray against temptations. Read your Bible regularly! As much as possible, avoid sin and avoid strife! Peace!

CONCLUSION

In conclusion, as we come to the end of this 21-day journey of miraculous prayer for liberation and deliverance, we stand on the precipice of divine transformation.

Throughout these sacred days, we have opened our hearts to the power of prayer, surrendering ourselves to the divine presence that resides within and around us. In this surrender, we have found liberation and deliverance from the chains that once bound us.

The benefits we have reaped from this miraculous prayer journey are beyond measure. Our spirits have been ignited with a newfound passion for life, as we have witnessed the manifestation of miracles in our lives.

Through our unwavering faith and devotion, we have experienced freedom from the burdens that weighed heavily upon us, be it fear, doubt, or past traumas. We have embraced a renewed sense of purpose and clarity, guided by the divine wisdom that has unfolded before us.

As we look back on these 21 days, we see the tapestry of our lives interwoven with threads of healing, restoration, and empowerment. Our relationships have been mended, forgiveness has flowed freely, and love has blossomed where it once withered.

The 21 Days Powerful Miraculous Prayer

We have discovered the strength within us to overcome adversity and face challenges head-on, knowing that we are divinely supported every step of the way.

But our journey does not end here. It is merely the beginning of a lifelong partnership with the divine.

As we continue to walk this path of liberation and deliverance, let us carry the lessons and blessings of these 21 days in our hearts.

Let us remain steadfast in our commitment to prayer, for it is through prayer that we unlock the door to miracles.

In the days, weeks, and years to come, let us remember the transformative power of prayer. Let us keep our hearts open to receive divine guidance, and our minds attuned to the whispers of the Universe.

May our lives be a testament to the miracles that are possible when we align ourselves with the highest good.

As we close this sacred chapter, let us embrace the liberation and deliverance we have found and extend it to others. Let us become beacons of hope and agents of change, sharing the transformative power of prayer with those who seek liberation from their own chains.

May this book serve as a constant reminder that miracles are not just distant possibilities, but living realities that can be experienced in our daily lives.

The 21 Days Powerful Miraculous Prayer

With faith as our compass and prayer as our vehicle, we embark on a journey of boundless miracles, where liberation and deliverance are forever within our reach.

Believe, dear reader, for your prayers have been heard, and miracles are unfolding even now.

With love and blessings,

Onuorah Chukwuemeka

PRAYER GUIDE PLANNER

TIMETABLE

As you journey into your total liberation and deliverance through these prayers. It is important to take record and evaluate yourself on your day-to-day activities.

DAYS	ACTIVITIES	REMARKS

The 21 Days Powerful Miraculous Prayer

The 21 Days Powerful Miraculous Prayer

The 21 Days Powerful Miraculous Prayer

The 21 Days Powerful Miraculous Prayer

The 21 Days Powerful Miraculous Prayer

The 21 Days Powerful Miraculous Prayer

The 21 Days Powerful Miraculous Prayer

The 21 Days Powerful Miraculous Prayer

If you have made it this far **Victory** is yours in Jesus Mighty Name.

Amen and Amen.

YOU ARE A WINNER

Printed in Great Britain
by Amazon